LAMENTATION

ADAM ROBERTS

LAMENTATION

IN THE STUART CROFT ARCHIVE

MA BIBLIOTHÈQUE

ADAM ROBERTS

LAMENTATION
IN THE STUART CROFT ARCHIVE

THE CONSTELLATIONS, BOOK XV

MA BIBLIOTHÈQUE, LONDON

 Published 2020

Printed by Printed World Publishing, Hastings, Great Britain

Set in Didot, Bodoni Ornaments

ISBN 978-1-910055-75-5

Papers used are from well-managed forests and responsible sources

MA BIBLIOTHÈQUE

For my mother and father, Hazel and Alan Roberts

CONTENTS

Lamentation
In the Stuart Croft Archive

Lamentation
In the Stuart Croft Archive

> Two prisoners whose cells adjoin communicate with each other by knocking on the wall. The wall is the thing that separates them but it is also their means of communication [...]. Every separation is a link.[1]

First Visit

I am sitting in the chill document room of the British Film Institute's National Archive. I have requested several boxes of papers that belonged to Stuart Croft. The boxes are a delight: a gentle grey exterior, a pale chalky interior, their folding design simple and yet precise. The manufacturer proudly stamps their mark into the very fabric of the acid-free card. These are boxes made to last. Inside them are the papers and notebooks of the film-maker and artist Stuart Croft.

Croft died suddenly on 14 March 2015. He was forty-four years old. His papers have been lodged here in Berkhamsted for safekeeping and study.[2] Stuart Croft died just a few months before Chantal Akerman, another film maker and artist, born in Brussels. I had organised in London a complete retrospective of her work, as part of my curatorial project called *A Nos Amours*, co-founded with Joanna Hogg in 2013. Akerman took her own life, a shock to her many admirers, myself included. Her charisma was undeniable, her reputation towering.

I was now looking at Stuart Croft's papers, a decision made in the aftermath of Akerman's death. My intention was to spend time absorbed in the surviving papers and records of an artist filmmaker, in an effort of discover something of the nature of loss and the value of memorialisation. What exactly disappears, and what survives? What is the afterlife of an artist?

Croft made films. And he made films which seem, at first glance, to be films about films. He made films that evoke other films, recreate other films, refer to other films, though they may be films that have never existed. His films were made to be played looped in galleries, not in the cinema auditorium. All the same, his work is imbued with a love and knowledge of cinema. I came to his films as one who also loves cinema, who revels in its potential to provide an aid to thought and a lexicon of emotions. I detect in Croft's work not only interest in art cinema, but also great delight in the gaudy flourishes of popular cinema, and even commercial advertising. All these are points of departure. It is impossible when looking at Croft's work not to mentally make note of films he must have had in mind as he devised and invented his clever and crystalline forms.

For me, another point of departure is to ask if Stuart Croft's project was at heart driven by a structuralist or, instead, a post-modern sensibility. That is to say, ask if his work builds forms from materials to hand, to be understood chiefly as a matter of design and of formal constraint. Or does instead his interest lie in quotation, with surface, and ironic detachment? To propose such a dichotomy may be useful, just as it had been helpful in the past when thinking about Chantal Akerman to explore the tension between her astute psychological realism in contrast to her formalist tendency. Here now, I set up questions that may enable first steps to be taken. Work in the archive is, with its partial records and its disorder, unlikely to give rise to easy interpretation. It is important to allow for opposing ideas, for ambivalence to thrive.

This place, this room at the National Archive, is unusual; it is not made with the comfort of the researcher in mind. Here it is cold, and in this winter of 2018 and 2019, very cold. Moreover, the table on which documents must be examined is situated in a room completely removed from the community of librarians. Security arrangements mean that even toilet visits and canteen breaks are policed. I am not made to feel at home, but then this is not a home. It is a depository of relics of the dead. It is a place where the physical remains of spent lives are kept, at least of those lives deemed significant enough to be worthy of retention. The documents are afforded the care and diligence that human remains, in decent societies, must be given. I ask about gloves, but the rule now is that clean hands are better than lint gloves, whose fibres are destructive.

I untie ribbon and open a box. I unfold card folders and look for the first time at Stuart Croft's hand writing. Here are his annotated scripts, his diaries and notebooks, his drafts for talks and lectures, his work-in-progress, his slides and documentation. These are the manuscript traces of his work and life. May I take pictures without flash? I may, though the Stuart Croft Foundation will need to approve any use.

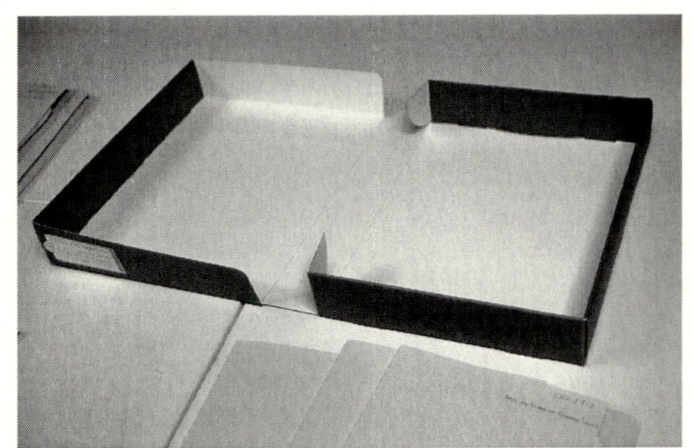

[fig. 1]

The physical traces of his life lie before me. Indeed, it was Stuart Croft's own hand that made these marks, the pressure of his pen on the paper that indents, sometimes lightly, sometimes so heavily as to tear the surface. This handwriting, these visible and lively marks, made by one no longer living, calls forth the presence of a hand that still writes, that writes constantly and forever, as if the dead had been summoned and cannot die. They are evidence of the uncanny.

Freud wrote about the uncanny, what in the German is *das Unheimliche*, thinking initially about dolls and waxworks, made in the image of the human. He talks about the dread that the dead might come to take us away, of the potent otherness of a double, a not-me that is me, from the other side of death. The not-me haunts, suggesting only too vividly the inevitable fate of all living beings.

Yet here in the chilly archive I resist such spooking, for the mark I see and the hand that I imagine are in truth forlorn—unique and poignantly lost. This is an unrepeatable gesture, lost in time. Each mark has no double, no simulacrum creeping up, glimpsed in the corner of my eye. Even if I make a photograph of that mark, the image is flat and distant. The marks exist as something in their own right, stubbornly so. Their physical presence, their sheer isolation, invokes for me a vivid sense of the moment of their making, the most idle and formless of them, the doodles and random hatching, most of all. Are they here and now, in the moment that I look at them, or else then and there, in the moment of their making? I am simply unable to locate them. They hover just beyond me and my moment, indeed they might be in another time frame.

Their effect on me is also an effect of their being unique, of their solitude in an age of reproduction. The marks are lonely.

All the same, the doodles, the marginalia, the crossings out, the marks of hesitation, are evidence of a mind caught in the act of changing, of its sudden shifts in understanding, of moments of insight, or of simple frustration. This is evidence, in physical form, of an active mind, a mind glimpsed like a fish breaking the surface in a river, sudden proof of another realm. Legible writing, writing that must be read, is never eloquent in such vein. More than this, these marks are authentic, precisely because they cannot be read and understood.

I am reminded of Neolithic cave painters who spattered pigment to make silhouettes of their own hands. The meaning of such images may be lost, yet they span the millennia, suggesting strongly the presence of the artist. The physical gestures that produced such a hand image are instantly guessed at or imagined. How the pigment glistens in the dim light of a taper, how the droplets sparkle, not yet dry! When I look at Croft's doodles and deletions I imagine the impatient jitter of a hand and the pen it holds, marking the paper, just as I imagine a Neolithic artist, paint in mouth, leaning to spit and sputter across their hand laid flat across a stretch of rock. When that is done, the hand is withdrawn to reveal a sign that we read millennia later.

The marks are stubborn. To me they are accusations, physically present, unassailable and inviolable. Stuart Croft may be gone, but these markings, inscribed or incised into the very fabric of the paper, assert themselves. I am here!—they seem to say.

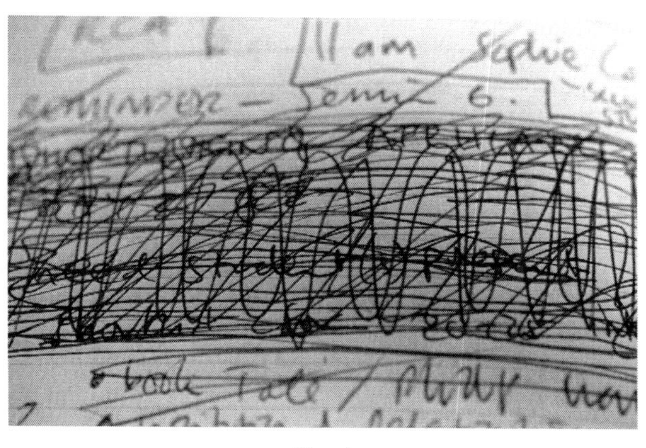

[fig. 2]

A connection to the films Stuart Croft made occurs to me, concerning their apparent referential quality. His films suggest to me that there is a precursor, something referred to, which should be familiar. He made spoof adverts for products that did not exist, or idents for imaginary brands, but in an idiom that I feel I know. He made dramatic films, with the sound and feel of cinema that seem very familiar, such as Hollywood musicals or *film noir.* Film allusions spring to mind, only to fade, because these works are made at a slight remove, inviting recognition and yet withholding it. They play at the margins of the mind. There is an equivocation between availability and unavailability. Croft makes use of the means and stylisations that we know well: of continuity editing, of the system of editing between different shot sizes, of the lexicon of action and gesture, and their permissible combinations. The scripts themselves—their plots and stories, the situations and the characters—draw on archetypical narratives, some from fable and romance, others from genre and well-worn narrative cinema situations. The forms therefore seem familiar, but they are always unstable, because their ready categorisation is undermined. The scenes may look familiar, and yet they never quite are. The anxiety this produces in me is the anxiety of being out of one's depth, about longing for something lost, always absent, about the distant unattainable object of love. These are scenes played looped, so whatever closures we may long for are denied.

The Stuart Croft Foundation has carefully gathered these papers and records, to create this archive. This is a project born out of love and respect, and must have involved a concerted effort. I am moved by the thought. I imagine a community whose numerous tender hands have sorted and assembled these materials, before at last tenderly enclosing them in these folders and safe boxes.

My engagement with these papers and my taking notice of the marks, and my photographing them, is now too a part of that performance of love, in keeping with the ageless rituals of love and respect, in this secular space which nevertheless reveals in its silence a temple-like aspect. I am become a priest of love.

Lamentation

Between 2013 and 2015, with my friend Joanna Hogg, I curated a complete retrospective of Chantal Akerman's films, and an exhibition of the greater part of her art work. Tragically, the retrospective reached its end just as news came of her death. It was a death by suicide. Such a death, her death, was a deeply traumatic event in my life, which took me by surprise, leaving me confused and depressed. Time passed, and I wondered about how to better understand and come to terms with this loss, for Akerman and her work had come to loom very large in my life.

I asked myself, if in order to undertake the work of mourning, indeed to come finally to accept the death of any loved one, to salve the acute pain of separation from a significant other, from those whose lives and opinions matter deeply, will it always be necessary to come to forget that other, to wait for erasure of vivid and acute memory, so that there might be a dimming of the clear mental pictures that are so much a part of a lived experience of the other? Must I pray for a time when I can no longer bring the other readily to mind, not hear that voice, not conjure its timbre and habits, be unable to recollect precisely the personality that was once so near and dear? And what, in the case of Akerman, of the body of work that persists, that can be experienced again at the click of a mouse, can be read about and discussed with others? Akerman herself appeared in many of her films, not as a scripted character, but as herself. Who and what is that person now?

Stuart Croft was never a performer in his work, and yet he was most certainly an author, a presence whose command animated all that is seen and heard. What is to be made of his absent presence now? Their legacies are being written, not now by them, but by others. Neither Akerman nor Croft may now be authors.

The opportunity to spend time in the National Archive, engaged in a close study of Croft's marks and traces, close to the tangible vestiges of his life and hand, might, I hope, lead me to some understanding of necessary forgetting, of how death transforms one kind of mark into another. Odd that they are experienced always in a present moment, as they are there on the table before me, yet are marks made historically. They are in some sense diminishing objects passing ever more remotely into history, like a departing train, shrinking into the distance. What can be gleaned from this passage from presence to absence, from their finally slipping away when closing folders and boxes at the end of every archive visit?

Might this study become a preoccupation that can displace the ineluctable presence of Chantal Akerman?

Might the work of mourning Akerman be hastened by contemplation of Croft's absence? Might one void help me come to terms with another?

Finally, might I come to an awareness of my relationship with all that is gone, with the community of the dead generally, with all those who have lived and made marks, glimpse perhaps what it means to be here now, the heir of all who have gone before, of all those who have made my moment what it is? That this building was built by others, planned by others, lit and facilitated by means of services put in place by others, is undeniable. I do not know them, and yet they are necessarily present, many of them long gone.

More directly, I am defined by my mother and my father, and their innumerable ancestors. Indeed, I am defined by all those who have lived before me, by the entire species, by their collective speaking and dreaming, a symphony of voices and lives, that weaves the warp and weft of my mind and thought. That is a community whose deeds and misdeeds define my sense of self, have produced my identity, just as their questioning and the answers they settled on have defined my prejudices and assumptions. I am certainly not an agent in the performance of myself. If I live, it is as a summation of all else.

In this moment, seated in this cold archive, I am a nexus, attempting to forge a link between past and future. If I fail, it will not matter, for others will follow. At least my search may provide some solace of my own, that will allow me to take a step forward into my own future, a step that will seem secure. I will have done with the past, and begin to face forwards.

I think of a Neolithic cave painter, whose name is unknown, and unknowable. And yet their hand, stencilled on rock, sends a blazing signal across time, to me. I hear that signal and, in its humility and brazen simplicity, understand that it speaks on behalf of all humanity, for the unremarked multitudes whose lives far outnumber the memorialised few, who share in a body just like that, which asserts simply that a name does not matter. All of us share and are embodied by that cave image of a hand.

However, the question for now, in this place, in this archive, is what I think of these marks on the page before me, whose maker is no more. And what of Stuart Croft's body of work, stored even now on shelves nearby, on hard drives and film emulsions, existing only in a state of potential being, for they require projection to become animated and visible? The fate of moving-image work generally must be uncertain, because to be seen they require installation and exhibition. Their voyages through time, unlike that of the Neolithic hand, require that they be presented, which is to presume that they are prized to be so privileged, so that the technology necessary has also been preserved. Their voyage through millennia cannot be so stealthy and so silent.

To remember necessitates forgetting. To remember any one thing must be to make a selection, and so to forget other things. To be able to remember all, as Jorge Luis Borges so dourly relates in *Funes el memorioso*,[3] must result in a forlorn retreat into an unlit room, in an attempt to remember less. What Funes remembers is infinite and unrewarding. Unsurprisingly, he died young.

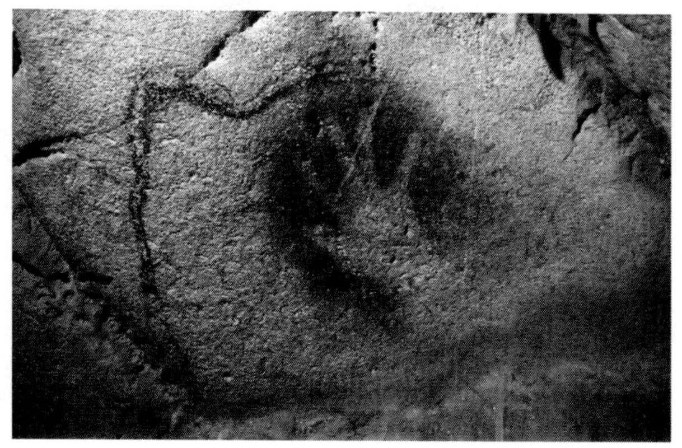

[fig. 3]

Physical movement is analogous. To move from one place to another is to lose direct contact with where once one was, to be awash with new sensations and new sights. Where once one was must now be remembered, if at all possible. Novelty erases, and memory must make do with outlines. A *madeleine* may provide a passing stimulus, but the work of recollection is at best partial. Even to turn back, to look back along one's path to the now distant place where once we stood, is to discover that it has become small. Distance and optics annihilate as much as time. Only in the archive do we believe that time and distance are denied their inevitability. However, just as the fossil record is a marvellously haphazard record of life, so the contents of an archive are contingent, all that is there the result of accident. Fossils and archives alike depend on researchers, without whom there can be only silence.

Distance

News from home is a film by Chantal Akerman.[4] It is a film made out of views of the city, what might be called general views, of the streets, pavements, and subway stations. At the start, sounds of the city are heard, but then Akerman's voice emerges, reading letters her mother has written to her from a distant home in Brussels. For the most part the city sounds rumble and stir politely in the background, but then at times rise up to drown out Akerman's murmuring voice. Watching this film is chastening because I myself did not keep letters that my own mother wrote to me, letters much like Akerman's. At the time, I thought them trivial. Watching this film, I see that I had been wrong. Akerman's mother had written to make anxious enquiry, to share details of the minutiae of family life, to give homely advice, and issue strict maternal commandments. The letters embody Akerman's relationship with her mother; their honesty and humanity undeniable. They bind and they nourish, even if at times they must have felt stifling; they are reassuring just as much as they may have been, at times, intolerable. That a relationship could find such affecting expression in commonplace writing was a humbling surprise. Akerman brilliantly understood the value of what others might discard. Out of shards and fragments, something enduring is made.

The film offers a pairing of mother and daughter, of mother's words and daughter's voice, of present performance and past inscription. It is a dialogue between the words spoken by the one on behalf of the other, between one place and other. Poignantly, it is a call without a response. The words, blended with city sounds seem mortared into the concrete and brick of the city. They are located, pinned to the place, and so unable to rise into the air and bridge the ocean that separates. Akerman's murmured recitation, so close and private, is a plain-chant, a search for comfort, proof only of yearning and unanswered need. The fragile murmur produces an oscillation between a fervent hope that what is distant may yet be present, and a fear that what is present only proves that all else is unattainable.

The closing shot of *News from home* is a view from a ferry, as it leaves Manhattan, looking back. The city skyline diminishes and shrinks. Mist blurs the familiar outline. The shot runs on, to last more than ten minutes.

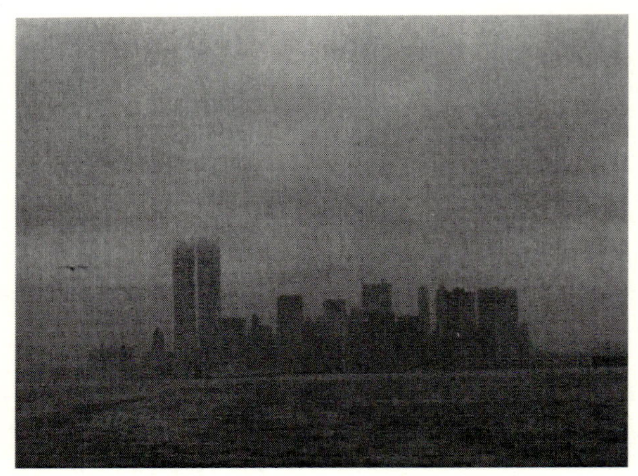

[fig. 4]

It prompts the thought that retrospection might be understood as a form of sight. It may be necessary to go to the ends of the earth to discover the extent and nature of tender regard, for without separation there is no pressing need to speak of love. Distance and loss, so to speak, are the roots of a poetics of love.

Beethoven's song cycle *An die ferne Geliebte* is said to be the first song cycle of the long tradition of German lieder. It begins by asserting the coincidence of distance and longing, of a sentiment refined by absence:

On a hill I sit, gazing
Into the hazy blue distance,
Towards far away pastures
Where, my beloved, I found you.[5]

Distance, this says, adds not just refinement to love, the hazy distance and the far away pastures are the embodiments of love itself. The hazy blue distance (*'Das blaue Nebelland'*) is a place, whose remoteness becomes a vanishing point in the poet's mind. Proximity would diminish the poignancy of the poet's love; separation from the object of love is essential.

The troubadours, poet/singers of medieval Europe, knew this well. In their lyrics, the poet typically suffers by being removed from the beloved. Anguish and longing are characteristic of love. The object of love is often aloof, disdainful or unobtainable, which calls forth song and poetry; to achieve the object of one's love would call forth nothing. Without distance and separation there would be no need of poetics. The distant beloved must vanish always into the blue hazy distance. The beloved is idealised, represented in terms of distance, virtue, and reputation. Absence makes the heart not only grow fonder, but makes possible love in the first place.

To reify a single point of view, and to organise perception and reality around such a point defines objects in terms of their apprehension: to be is only ever to be perceived. It follows then that if to love is to perceive, then the poet of love is necessarily a poet always alone. The lyricist is confronted by an ocean, whose heaving dangerous expanse, whose dark depths make any voyage perilous, annihilation inevitable. Time and tide make trivial the lone voice. All that the poet can do is gaze out across the sea:

> I'll sing, sing *lieder*,
> Lamenting my agony![6]

Beethoven's song pinpoints a passive acceptance of separation, just as Akerman can murmur only in invocation of her mother, and now, in this archive, boxes and folders keep safe the marks and inscriptions of a departed artist. The living must hold on to what they can, looking always to the other shore.

I sit looking at Stuart Croft's diaries. Poignantly, he made entries for appointments beyond the date of his sudden death. What is the status of such an appointment? Is it simply posthumous? Or is there a more exact term? Later on, the diary pages are vacant. Having leafed through the diaries, year by year, month by month, this is a true silence, a poignant assertion of the silence of death. This visit is at an end.

The Next Visit

To approach the document room at Berkhamsted it is necessary to pass through the film print despatch area. Here are stacked many film cans, a few from their vast collection, awaiting dispatch to cinematheques the world over. They are heavy, bulky, and valuable. Despite the rise of the digital format, film prints are prized, and huge costs run up in order to share these precious few copies. I notice Derek Jarman's *Blue,* Leone's *Once Upon a Time in America*, and Rossellini's *Stromboli*. I sigh for the past of this already aged art form, with its rituals and its ongoing loss of itself. The sounds and images of these films must now survive, if they can, amid a vast proliferation of image- and moving-image making, in an age from which former hierarchies of value have been eradicated. It is not now the case that these films, once widely regarded as canonical, can take that standing for granted.

Sight of these rusting film cans is nevertheless suggestive to me of their potential, for they have in the past overwhelmed my senses and may do so again. Not only I, but others have converged—will converge—on cinemas where these objects are unveiled. We sit meekly while the machines necessary for the ritual are powered and animated, their cogs and shutter mechanisms turning and fluttering, their blinding light unveiled and cast upon a screen. We are attentive as in front of us something marvellous happens. We know that these projections are the sacraments of the art, and we its devotees! Our eyes are suitably upcast, for we are before our God. We are filled with a sense of our own passing; we know that this time is limited, that this film print is fragile, that this art form all but faded. We would not have it any other way, for we are a cult of the ruin. Such sepulchral thoughts are inevitable in the archive.

The boxes I have requested for this second visit include scripts for several of Croft's films. He reworked them constantly, as the heavy presence of deletion, mark-up and marginalia confirm. Croft was working in relation to cinema films that he knew well. His references are eclectic, embracing contemporary Hollywood as much as the canonical works of world cinema. He wanted to make films that made use of the technology and idioms of commercial cinema, and weave out of these appropriations and reconfigurations looped dramatic situations that would play endlessly. His scripts show him labouring to find and refine nuances that would lend his works the atmosphere, the strangeness, the poised and timeless quality that is so striking in his work.

But his film references are elusive. Specific sources may be guessed at, because their style and manner, gesture and idiom, seem so often familiar. Yet, as with the film stills created by Cindy Sherman, it is not possible to specify which film in particular is invoked. As with pastiche, genre is imitated, yet also like parody these are works that make play with their appropriations.

In order to prepare for this visit I had looked at two of the films: *Comma 39* of 2011 and *The Stag Without a Heart* of 2010.

The first, *Comma 39*, is a dance film. Notes made by Stuart Croft say that this is a dance between, 'an aristocratic beauty and a wounded man'.[7] It is an 'endless dance of desire and betrayal'. The wounded man here has a disfigured mouth, perhaps an extreme effect of stroke, or of an accident involving fire. She is in chiffon, an off-the-shoulder veil fluttering in a light breeze. He is in a dinner suit with a bow tie. The set is pink and rose, gathered curtains hang backstage beyond a set of steps. The sound track is made of soaring string sounds, with tympani beating out a staggered warning. The choreography is balletic, the pair generally at close quarters, though when the mood darkens, they separate. There is a gun, perhaps so that beauty may kill the beast. She resists a dance of supplication, an ardent solo from the wounded man. The camera faithfully tracks the movement, though the viewer is brought up short from time to time by sight of off-stage machinery: a wind machine, coiled scenery ropes, and lighting rigs. Artifice and the conventions of the Hollywood musical are alluded to, then jettisoned. Inspiration for the imagery of this work must include the Broadway Melody ballet in *Singin' in the Rain*, in which Cyd Charisse and Gene Kelly glide about on a vast pastel sound stage.[8] Significantly, Charisse wears a long chiffon scarf that is lifted by an artificial breeze, an image of otherworldliness.

The Stag Without a Heart presents a dramatic scene, set in a room reminiscent of Citizen Kane, vast and oak-panelled.[9] A gaping open fireplace leers like an entrance to the underworld. This is a bedroom, and a man sits on the edge of an empty bed, addressing his speech to the pillow, as if there were a child lying there to listen to his tale. The man is dressed formally, perhaps about to go to dinner.

The story he is telling is an ancient fable, as told by Aesop but adapted by Croft. In Aesop's version, a stag is lured to a lion's den, and eaten. A fox, who had lured the stag with the promise of kingship, stealthily ate the heart and lied to the lion that the stag had had no heart. A tale then with a clear-cut ending. Stuart Croft now adapts the tale, so that the stag's heart is first torn out then put back. A grim tale, stripped of the closure of Aesop. Looping the film now means that bloody murder and resurrection must continue forever.

What is the tone of this piece? Is this man, dressed in evening wear, the epitome of civilised menace perhaps? Indeed, music underlines and accentuates the tale's sinister turns, like a coil of smoke that shrouds the devil. Yet this is also a comforting scene, redolent of bed time, in which a sleepy, beloved child detains his parent to tell yet again this favourite tale. The parent is unwearied, and the film plays endlessly, in a loop.

We, the viewers of Croft's gallery work, may listen to this tale over and over again, safely tucked up in bed, as it were, sleepy and beginning to dream. The film may be experienced as an incantation, casting its spell out of patterned repetition and withholding of closure. We may presume much about this situation, but no firm conclusion can follow. The details (the costume, the setting, the situation) invoke thoughts of other films, or rather the ghosts of other films, that may be guessed at, suspected, and worried about. These are films glimpsed in the corner of the eye; they haunt by their very absence.

The story told has its origins in folklore, that realm in which animals may talk, where telling and retelling have made normal the impossible. There is comfort to be found in these recitations, in the rhythms of the narrative, in the ritualised delivery, even if we are hearing of a heart torn from a living being. This is the formless moment of falling asleep, suspended between the waking world and the dream world to come. In the cinema auditorium, in the dark, lost in the moment, where we are so often brought to that same half-wakeful state, where repetition and the familiarity of familiar faces and situations allows for a lovely loss of concentration, knowing all the same more or less just where we are, and what to expect. We are lulled into a contented state of *déjà vu*, as if lost in time. Here the end may precede the beginning, and all our dreams can come true. Time may be suspended, or disappear altogether. It seems to me that Stuart Croft alludes to that happy space, and then darkens it, filling it with phantoms. His incorporation of the past into the present spooks me, a chilling reminder that so much of what I am and what I can know is out of awareness.

Returning to the archive, the mismatch between Stuart Croft's precise, carefully made films, and these dog-eared notebooks and diaries, these sheaves of torn, marked pages, these vestiges of work and deliberation, strike home. Woe fills me. I close up the boxes and make a hasty retreat.

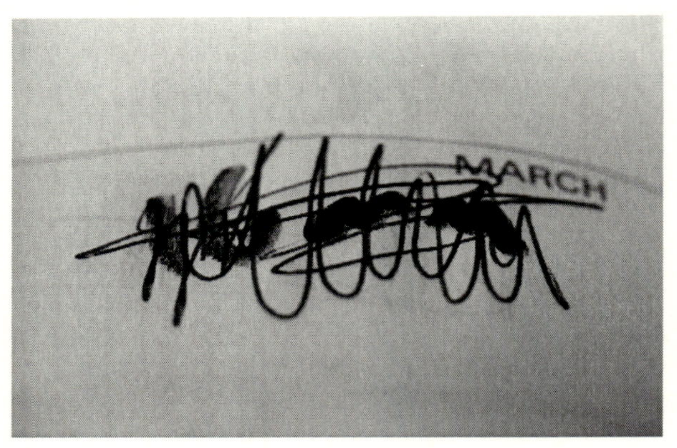

[fig. 5]

Residue

A residue is something left over, which remains after some process, perhaps of evaporation or of wearing away. Residues may be revealing, a step towards discovery, a revelation of constituent elements or underlying forms. Yet residue also speaks of a prior state, one that has been disrupted, one no longer whole and intact. A residue is the resolution of prior potential, in one direction only. A residue may provide for the discovery of a hidden nature, but something essential must be lost. It must be as if Schrödinger's cat has been let out of its box.

Death has stilled the action of Stuart Croft's hand; he can no longer add to this finitude of marks and traces. When the National Archive received his papers, they accepted a residue, that they pledge to preserve, as far as possible, in perpetuity. Here before me is tangible proof of that compact.

These papers on the table are present, yet they are also a bridge to their past. The marks were made, I can see, by the pressure and dexterity of his hand, a moment now vividly existing in my mind. I am, as I lean closer, both in this my own moment of looking, but also now a witness to the moment of their making. I delight in this intermediate moment, poised between the life and vividness of my own sensorium in the presence of the living, writing artist. Without then my noticing, I slip out of my own time and place, to look down upon a hand not my own. The marks on the page are a talisman, bringing me into presence of this other living hand, that hovers over the page, the ink glistening, not yet dry. This is Stuart Croft's hand. In that moment, my hand has become his hand. Yet this moment of mystery cannot last, for in the end the mark recedes to join again its fraternity. I am cast out.

This moment cannot know what future is being made. I sift and I sort, I rearrange and juxtapose. The papers and notebooks emit their dry sounds, a breath of sorts. My fingertips make soft contact, as if to read braille. The paper is not yet brittle, the state of inevitable yellowing and dried-out fragility far off. The imprint and weight of Stuart Croft's pen bearing down on the paper is perceptible, not least under a raking light. It is as if he has left the room, just for a moment, and I await his return. I have taken his place, sit in his chair, have laid his pen down to my right. It is as if the marks had been made by me, and I am now pausing before writing once again.

To be here, posthumously, is a prelude to my speaking in valediction. It is my duty to devise a gesture that can make a signal towards the future in which Stuart Croft's legacy will reside. The body of his work will be thus carried forward into the future, in a ceremony that transforms the outline of a man into a constellation, a set of points, a heavenly figure. I am a boatman to port the soul of Stuart Croft across the river of forgetfulness to what lies beyond.

The conceit fades and I am again in a cold room, aware of the silence. The sarcophagi, the boxes, must be closed and returned, to be replaced on their allotted shelves. Yet as I gently fold back pages and pack the boxes I fall upon a letter, dated 2001, in rejection of an application for funding. I feel a pang of sympathy:

> Thank you for your application to the Digital Tales Scheme. Unfortunately, the selection panel were unable to recommend your project, MILK, for funding in this round of awards. Due to the high volume of applications, we are unable to provide individual feedback regarding your project.[10]

Many must know what it is to receive such a letter. I certainly have a great number of my own. Circumstances vary but the pang is a familiar experience that must lie in wait for those that make applications for support and funding. This is a moment shared, linking the past with the present, but it slips back into a sea of generalisations, like fish caught but slipping the hook. I make the photograph and depart.

Futurisation

If this is a word, then it must mean something about an act of bringing into an up-to-date state, or into a state suggestive of how it may yet be. It suggests that there is agency, rather than a future into which all are passively conveyed. There is a suggestion too of a direction of travel, from the past towards the future. Work in the archive might be thought of in this way. Traces and marks made in the past must be recorded, ordered, indexed, and placed into sequence. The facility to do this requires an active agency. The agency of the researcher in the archive is to hold the pieces in place, to pin them down, to box them, to provide reassurance, and then to convey them safely into the future. Ideally, they are made fit for the future.

Texts from antiquity were all but lost, only to be recovered and happily read again. It is sobering that so much was lost, so little saved. For this reason, a sense of loss haunts the contemporary imagination, because we claim continuity with the cultures of the past. We have sprung from those ruins. Any archivist regards documents, however fragmentary, as treasures of infinite fragility and infinite value. The archival urge is powerful.

Long before our contemporary discovery of mass extinction, such as that at the close of the Permian, or that now in progress, the ruins of the ancient world defined the imagining of collapse and demise. The past was uncertain, or at least proved that vanity is always punished, that greatness is provisional. As Shelley's poem *Ozymandias* can say, 'Round the decay / Of that colossal Wreck, Boundless and bare / the lone and level sands stretch far away'.[11] Time is the leveller. This can be a poem devoid of anxiety, despite its contemplation of annihilation, for though time brings down the colossus, life goes on, even if transformed. The discovery of deep time and the possibility of extinction make such a sanguine view less available.

Archaeology is a performance, in which the depositions of time are brushed away to reveal a forgotten past, onto which may be projected our contemporary hopes and fears. Inscriptions and literatures may be deciphered and rediscovered, presented in definitive scholarly editions, in which interpretation is made secure, cross indexed and lent authority, standing in sharp contrast with the provisional present, the unreliable and ever-shifting contingent present. The silence of the tomb, the eloquence of ruins, their weight and command, is a comfort, above all, in the face of the unknowable future. To catalogue the past, to archive its traces, is work that secures ourselves, establishing security amid the instability of the moment. The silence of the library and the archive are comforting bastions against entropy and loss. Work in the archive is work that can secure the future.

If futurisation is possible, it will require a ritual. I wonder if my visits should be determined by arcane methods, such as the lunar calendar, or if I should ablute. At the very least, I am not to use ink, writing my notes in pencil only. I am polite and careful, and approach the boxes with respect. I make no loud noises near them, nor any sudden movement. I take to murmuring.

Forgetting

Remembering well demands that something be lost. It is not enough to recollect a detail without making a selection, without prizing one thing over another. To turn a particular memory over in the mind demands its isolation from others that would render it unremarkable. The outlines of a buried form, either as a fossil or an archaeological remain, demands excavation and disposal of concealing top soil. Layers of rock and sediment above the stratum in question are discarded, and careful brushing brings to light the impression of something that once lived. The work of identification and taxonomy may begin.

Who decides what is to be forgotten, and what

remembered? This sifting, this determination of what is to be said and not said, of which sign is to have power and which not, is surely a priestly role, for this work may be given only to the guardians of a mystery. Only the initiated may approach the holy of holies, only the elect enter the sanctuary, only the chosen stand close to and know the mind of the Godhead. But proximity is dangerous, for to be close in this way is to pose a potential threat. Performances and gestures must be devised, orders of service authorised. A priestly caste is called for, mitigating the risk of harm, observing the rules of cleanliness, banishing misunderstanding, placing precisely forms into their proper relationships. This is the highest calling.

It is the task and responsibility of the archivist to choose which documents and relics history will access. So too the researcher must make choices and discard as much as is found. The act of creating an index, the imposition of a system of dating, the proper notation of contexts, however hesitant or provisional, is a decisive gesture. It may be irreversible. In the case of the papers in front of me, the selection of which papers would be kept and then put into boxes has been done by others. This researcher begins work in a realm whose mapping has already begun, whose reimagining may require the destruction therefore of preconceived notions, damage that may be inadvertent. It is work that is possible only because prior work has been done.

It is impossible, excited by thoughts of lost works from the ancient world, not to imagine that there may exist dozens of surviving documents not listed here in the archive index, perhaps in hidden boxes and secret compartments of cabinets stored in other places. Perhaps they were inadvertently consigned to the flames. What voice or voices go unheard? They are a ghostly crowd who gather to shuffle endlessly at the shoulder of the researcher, their powers of speech muted and faint, yet collectively uniting as if to be heard, insisting that they too have a story. Impossible not then to look anxiously over-shoulder and be surprised that one sits alone, despite the clamour.

For any who visit the archive, to sift and sort, to question and make notes, to assess and reassess, to read and read again, it is an ardent hope that a narrative be found, perhaps by the discovery of connections between elements, that others might not have seen. The placing of pottery shards into sequences, by the attentive noting of subtle points of similarity and dissimilarity, is one of the most powerful archaeological tools, able to produce stable chronologies for lost cultures. By such deft methods patterns emerge. Genealogies may then be confirmed, victories and defeats dated, lost societies made visible and live again in the imagination. All is purpose and method, and the navigation sure-handed. Wild shores and nameless lands are made tame.

The Limbic Brain

Stuart Croft gave a talk at Middlesex University:

> But it is important to me because the viewer is denied information, at the same time as information is being offered up. The film is edited as a loop, it joins onto itself, we can walk in and enter it at any moment in the gallery.[12]

He is talking about *Loss Leader*, which he first exhibited in 2000. This appears to be an advert for a car, the 'VXV', though this may be a literal reading as the work is a scattering of elliptical fragments. Stuart Croft appropriates the form of the 'sting' from the world of advertising, those condensed flourishes, often with punchy musical accompaniment, that are repeated *ad nauseam*. Such short logo-laden passages are intended to become ingrained and recognisable, identified with a product or service, as impossible to forget as a jingle on the mind, that annoyance sometimes called an earworm. *Loss Leader* presents short, fragmentary dramatic scenes. A woman looks at a transparency of a foetal scan, suggestive of conception. A bloody detail that cannot be placed is suggestive of birth. An aged man crawls like a baby, suggestive of first and last steps. These fragments burst out of darkness, which in the gallery space, is forceful. The fragments are loud and the flurries bright, but they are soon gone. The silence and the dark are a space for the dying down of an after-image, for a grasping towards meaning, or perhaps the failure to understand. These patterns are at best glimpsed, but, because they are made in the wake of the recognisable forms and methods of advertising, we feel an immediate familiarity. Our reaching hands, grasping in the dark, close tight and are rewarded–such joy!–by discovery of the familiar, that which we know, whose image and significance spring happily to mind.

We are well used to such fragmentary gestures, to these memetic flourishes of advertising, and have learned to grasp their mood and import in an instant. The human apparatus, of eye and brain, latches onto the rapid light show, the animation and busy fluctuation with greedy appetite. Reading of signs is a facility in which we revel, because it flatters the ego. It is a game that is its own reward. It may be the only novel characteristic of our modern mind, birthed as it has been in the shopping arcade, flitting from moment to moment, unfocused, given over to a fugue-like suspension of alacrity. The intermittent flicker of attention induces a contented yet receptive state of mind. 'The individual consciousness more and more secures itself in reflecting, while the collective consciousness sinks into ever deeper sleep'.[13]

As Croft launches his fleeting fragments, he trades, I believe, on just this facility. The intermittent presentation, which plunges the gallery visitor again and again into a darkness suffused with after-images, fragmented and unpredictable, refusing to propose a narrative, offering a tantalising series of signs, the reading of which must occur subliminally, and which negates the sense of the linear passage of time. Here the tick-tock does not count off, but signals—every time—the start.

Here is weightlessness and timeless suspension, a descent into the limbic brain, where the only values that matter are agreeable *versus* disagreeable, nice *versus* nasty. The limbic brain is associative, intrinsically emotional, a purring creature of comfortable inattention. In the dark especially, the thinking mind is lulled and submerged, dreams and fancies emerge, rising like whales out of the emerald depths. These slow-moving yet vast leviathans are reminders of eternity, their migrations and soundings mysterious, plumbing the depths of a measureless, unknowable realm. In this state of mind, presumably, we are most at the mercy of marketing, whose strategies seek always to supplant our desires. Stuart Croft well understands their method and brute force.

I am wrenched back into the present of the archive because the cold has numbed me and I must move my limbs. The inscriptions seem suddenly forlorn, a stark reminder of the fact that their maker is no more. I am now inattentive through cold. No mark speaks and sparkles on the page. I am filled with sorrow, thinking that whatever trace I linger over there can be no recapture of that which is lost, no recovery of lost time. Even these marks, palpable and vivid evidence of life, signalling eager anticipation across time, are but a looped animation of an ever fading moment, like the ever descending Shepard–Risset *glissando*, the most forlorn musical expression ever discovered. The sinking tones, trapped in a perpetual decline, are the embodiment of entropy, a sound that none may hear for long and stay sane. [14]

The pages and their marks are a snap-shot of a moment of disappearance, repeated endlessly as a set of missing moments—the Cheshire Cat who was here only a moment ago. To be in contact with the pathos of these now silent marks, invokes for me the pathos of all endings, not only that of Stuart Croft, but also that of Chantal Akerman, and of the multitude of endings than any life accrues. All time is lost and irrecoverable, every erasure, even if named and held in mind for as long as possible, is but a fading pattern in a faulty, stuttering recollection. The past is an after-image at best, a blur in the eye that becomes ever more formless and unrecognisable.

Leafing through albums, notebooks and diaries is like a vain reaching back into the dark recesses of a drawer that has not been opened for some long time, scraping and scratching with timid finger tips, in the hope that they may close at last on a lost object, whose form cannot be deduced by touch alone, and so provide for a moment of vivid anticipation. Yet then to bring this lost treasure into the light is invariably to know disappointment, for the unknown has an allure that cannot be bettered. 'Rosebud,' I murmur, reminded of Kane feeding, with his last breath, our belief in significance. What we presume to be Kane's last and only comfort is an object necessarily consumed in fire. All comforts are perishable, those residing in our memories most of all.

The rituals of remembrance are sincere; there is no decorum more carefully observed than that of the funeral. I think too of the solemn listing of the names of the departed on All Souls' Day, and the silence at the Cenotaph at the eleventh hour, each of them sacrosanct. Remembrance, it is clear, should be undertaken in decent and sombre fashion, in correctly hushed tones. These are the hallmarks of a culture that is in good health. The proper regard for the dead, if abandoned, is a sure prelude to barbarism.

We resist and dread the dark night closing in. We fear lightless places. We hate abandoned clearings in the forest overgrown and fast returning to the shade. We detest signs of growing disorder and the absence of any happy sign of cultivation. We long for good order, neatly clipped vines, evidence of organisation and care. We know that neglect signals all ends, and our own in particular.

We prefer the distant prospect because the near field can be disappointing, messy even: do not look too closely! *Et in Arcadia ego*.[15]

Chantal Akerman Again

The falling silent of Chantal Akerman was lamentable, for she was a beacon, an empowering presence for me and for many others. Her work had been so rich and very varied, her intelligence and vision celebrated by film-makers, artists, and in the academy.

At the age of twenty-four Akerman made a film that became a benchmark against which all other cinema would be measured: *Jeanne Dielman, 23, Quai du Commerce, 1080 Bruxelle*s. Her large body of work, spanning forty years, included film and art installations. Hers is not yet, however, a household name. It may be that her approach, and her themes, assume too much. Above all, she expects that we may be willing to feel and know abjection.

Her film *Histoires d'Amérique* was made in 1989.[16] It contains a scene which is for me the emblematic kernel of her project. Over a shot of the skyline of New York by night Akerman paraphrases a Hasidic story that has been told and retold by many, including Martin Buber and Elie Wiesel. This is Akerman's version:

> A rabbi always passed through a village to get to the forest, and there, at the foot of a tree (and it was always the same one) he began to pray

and God heard him. His son too always passed through the village but he could not remember where the tree was, and so he prayed at the foot of any old tree and God heard him. His grand-son did not know where the tree was, nor the forest, but went to pray in the village and God heard him. His great-grand-son did not know where the tree was, nor the forest, not even the village, but he still knew the words of the prayer, and so he prayed in his house and God heard him. His great-great-grand-son did not know where the tree, nor the forest, nor the village were, not even the words of the prayer, but he still knew the story and told it to his children; and God heard him.

It is a wonderful story, speaking cheerfully of the loss of language, of the erasure of comfort, meaning, and signification. It is, of course, a story that inevitably brings to mind the Shoah and the Jewish diaspora generally. This sense of inexorable loss of culture, history, and identity is delivered lightly, and with playful mischief. It is, however, a forlorn tale, however trippingly told. The story reveals how culture may be stripped back, and so all may be lost.

I suspect this story goes to the heart of the matter for Akerman, for so many in her family were murdered by the Nazis. Moreover, the Poland of her grand-mother had been razed to the ground, the obscure Yiddish variant of the shtetls of her ancestors consigned by the death camps to oblivion,[17] and the rituals of her surviving community now performed only in scattered corners of the globe. Her work must be understood in the context of such rupture and break. With the loss of so many any cultural transmission remains a miracle, let alone that abjection has not cast survivors irreparably into inertia and despair

To return to *News from home*, her film of 1977: for the soundtrack, as has been described, Akerman reads letters from her mother, letters replete with scraps of news from home. Akerman's voice struggles to be heard amid the din of the city. As the camera widens its view, to encompass the context of this city life, her voice grows faint. Distance silences, for the city, comprehended as a whole, is a wordless place. Individual voices and individual significance are annihilated: the city is vast, refusing to be encompassed, a vortex of collective purpose and intention, pushing out of earshot communication between a daughter and a mother.

That film's final shot, taken from the Staten Island Ferry, as it moves out onto the wide river, looking back towards Manhattan, presents an ever-widening view, revealing the scale of the city, driving home an awareness of separation and insignificance. The cries of a lone gull drive home a feeling of pathos.

The very act of seeking to encompass the city, the desire to reveal a context, is to become deprived of the possibility of contact. Signs of life are lost, to be replaced by silence. As the camera moves out and away, the city takes on the aspect of the mausoleum, the only sign of life the sentinel gull. As the shot rolls on, which it does for more than ten minutes, the city becomes unreadable, a misty generalisation, the thoughts and words of Akerman's mother a distant memory.

Akerman's Hassidic tale is a reminder of voices

lost in the Shoah, 'always that', as she lamented in her installation work *D'Est: au bord de la fiction* (1995). Her forest becomes my forest in which I am lost, and it is the context in which I visit the archive. To be among the carefully preserved remnants of work and life, among fragmentary remains, to be concerned with spectres is a lamentable project. Retrospection, inescapably, is an elegiac task.

Like the ruins of antiquity, the disaster of the Shoah prefigures the disaster yet to come. It commandeers and defines how I imagine the coming mass extinction at the end of the Anthropocene. The Shoah is a shadow that reaches out across the landscape of our imagination, the inescapable and dread index of human potential. It eradicates the past, and provides definition and meaning to the possible annihilation of all futures. The Shoah haunts our present, and makes ghosts of the living. It has been said that the Shoah 'lies outside speech as it lies outside reason',[18] proposing that the defining event of modern times may not be spoken of. Language has failed. It was into such a silence that Chantal Akerman was born. Her mother Natalia preferred to raise her daughters without speaking of her own experiences in the camps, hoping that this would spare them nightmares. But for a caring and attentive child such evasions are dreadful. Akerman called them *holes*, absences that came to define her work, perhaps limit her life.

The prelude to absence is loss, and in Akerman's films, a sense of loss is pervasive. Her mother's words in *News from home* are drowned out by city noise and lost as a boat leaves the city behind. In her most poignant work, her final film, *No Home Movie*, Akerman attends her sleeping mother whose old age and frailty are all too apparent. A year after Natalia died, Chantal ended her own life.

Anthropocene

We have named this era the Anthropocene, which brags that we have overwhelmed the natural world, and that we arrogantly or forlornly have defined its limits, for this act of naming defines an end as well as a beginning. It portends the death of language and our form of life. After we have gone, silence will fall. It is impossible not to relate such finality to the Nazi project, which was to annihilate a people and their culture, to impose a dread and final silence. In the terms of one we must comprehend the other.

Worst of all, it may well be a universal human urge that was exemplified by that Nazi dream, that is, the compulsion to master and conquer life itself, to humanise nature, to deny responsibility for the other. To valorise will and command, chaos is tamed, disorder made orderly, the forest cleared, and a stillness imposed, a stillness where none may speak, in which nothing may be implied, nothing be heard beyond an echo of the last command. No need then of expression, nor of metaphor; no further human tears need be shed, no feeling again be felt. Order and finality are achieved, a kind of peace.

The Nazis created copious records, fastidious archival proof of their atrocities, only then to burn and destroy them as best they could, adding a minor accretion of ash to the geological record, a trace of human purpose to be incorporated into the geology of earth. Overlaid onto this thin deposit, the Anthropocene will accrue a fatter, highly toxic, layer to that geological stratum. Our misdeeds then will form a part of the crystalline structure of the planet, a lasting and damning indictment.

To return to the closing shot of *News from home*: the camera is afloat, making a passage over water. It is a backward gaze, perhaps to suggest regret and resignation. What thoughts passed through Chantal Akerman's mind as her camera, surveying the receding city, a city where Jewish refugees and survivors found safety in which to flourish? Is that a city in which to recreate, for example, the forms of shtetl life, or instead a place where assimilation is pursued but at the risk of lost of identity and memory? Is that city a museum or a laboratory? The last shot of Akerman's film is in truth a blank canvas, on which may be inscribed hope as much as regret, despair or resignation. It is all things and nothing. It encompasses human language, it is a babble formed from all voices. But the single voice is lost, in particular that of a mother, asking if her daughter is getting enough sleep.

Natalia Akerman died in 2014. *No Home Movie* was to be her daughter Chantal Akerman's last film, released in 2015. The film is suffused with an astonishing tenderness, an all but unique document of the warp and weft of the relationship between mother and daughter. Their story is at its most luminous when the film-maker—the daughter—attends so simply to the peaceful sleep of her aged mother. Natalia's head lies tilted back, resting on a pillow, eyes shut, pulse visible under her skin. This is a life the Nazis tried to end, yet here now is a moment of caress in which we may all participate.

What is a researcher in the archive looking for? Perhaps the work is motivated by the mystery and challenge of partial traces, activating that human urge to uncover pattern, in a hungry longing for an unprecedented breakthrough? Or more modestly, is it to identify what will be useful to others, and so facilitate further research or support existing scholarship? The enigma of these marks and jottings seems to call, above all, for engagement of an active imagination, one that cannot help but envisage the hand that held and used a pen, that made marks and deleted them, that hesitated and overwrote. This is to discover sympathy between beings, that spans time, and so to make contact with lost life. It is work of looking closely, of coming into the presence of the lost other.

The gentle beholding of a mother's sleeping face, when the camera is placed so as to capture signs of breath and life, requires Natalia Akerman to have trust in her daughter, trust whose depth we can guess at because it is granted by one who is sleeping peacefully. This moment, given and received, is not an intrusion. The film is a form of archival gathering, a storing up of images for posterity. The grain store is filled to bursting, providing for the future. This film offers sight of a future, a future with the potential for life, for compassion and trust.

I hoped, thinking of this scene of Chantal Akerman recording her mother's sleeping face, to have found a way out of thoughts of the terminal, of annihilation. But comfort is denied me, in this Anthropocene Age, amid the destruction of the natural and the decline of diversity and extinction of species. I am trapped in the eddies of the Hudson River, unsure of my destination. I have only a retrospective view, and I cannot turn. The shot of the receding skyline never ends, because it is looped. The archive is a place that can offer only repetition, because it is intolerant of change.

Palaeontology

The archive is a rock face, layered, stratified and folded. Time is confused so that only the expert eye can determine true lineage. The fact that one layer is found one above another may mean the opposite of what we might lazily suppose. Geology is an unreliable witness. Marks and patterns in the stone remind us of the forms of living things, yet we should guard against unfounded assertion. As Edmund Gosse' father, Philip Gosse, insisted, these discoveries may be but a test of our faith set by the Creator.

It is no coincidence for me that Philip Gosse was the first to devise and build a seawater aquarium. His enclosure of sea life into a domesticated image of human control and supervision was the kind of abomination that only someone clinging to belief in the transcendent importance of Man [*sic*] could conceive. For me, the sea-water aquarium is a machine to make inert the magical power and supernatural effect of the sea. Ultimately, this aquarium enables atrocities to be committed elsewhere: the natural world may now safely be assaulted, for mastery has been demonstrated, nature encapsulated, and obliteration of the original can matter little if at all. The sea-water aquarium is an environment in a state of balance, whose keeper must measure exactingly the acidity, salinity, and the mineral composition of its waters, and make adjustments as necessary. The choice of life forms for this ark depends on whether they might consume one another, or their habits conflict with the requirements of the aquarium's master. The light is managed, the feed controlled, the aeration relentless. The purpose is display, and the gratification of the viewer. This is a form of slavery, an imposition of an order that denies the dignity of living things. Akerman's mother's sleeping face is its opposite.

With sour thoughts of Philip Gosse in mind, I conclude that my task in the archive is an imposition of a system of interpretation, the fixing with pins of beings into a defined, imposed order. This method obliges me to name parts, to make dissections, to reveal anatomy. I feel compassion for the objects of my study, and wish them free once more. Yet the relationship I have with these traces seems unstable. I am not even sure that we inhabit the same temporal frames, for we are in differing relativistic states. Our clocks are simply not synchronised.

I look at a mark, and hope to determine its value as it travels towards me through time, but find myself losing any possible sense of its place in my world. It is elsewhere, everywhere, nowhere. For reference, I have brought printed photographs of the silhouettes of a human hand made in the caves of Chauvet, and the cup and ring carvings at Cairnbaan, which were doubtless made to survive their makers.[19] These, for me, are totemic images, and I want to place them beside Stuart Croft's marks. These various remnants have travelled through time and meet here, so that together they may enter into a conference that spans all human history. A murmur rises from the images, as they begin their exchange. I am excluded, however, for I am the third, an interloper, because I am one of the living. My terms of reference are crude by contrast.

Not only am I excluded from this timeless exchange, but I reflect that even in my own era, the Anthropocene, an era of a compulsive and fecund making of documentation, photography, and recordings, we have created archives on a scale that cannot be imagined, that are already beyond our capacity for study and interrogation, at least not by those of us alive or even yet to be born. The vast accumulations of images, sounds, moments, and selves are beyond survey even by those busy making them. If a halt were called, it would take the innumerable generations past, present, and yet to come simply to play back or read that which is already on record. We are made small by the body of evidence stored, by which we will be judged.

A consequence of the scale of this archive is that what is conserved, however much loved, cherished, or respected, must then be indiscriminately stored. We document ourselves freely and openly, as if there is to be a future when the selection that flatters will be made. The fecundity of our making of signs is necessarily indifferent to the fact of the imminent silence, when none will survive to survey our colossal folly. Here are records of abuse, violence, killing, and torture, sitting in splendid democratic equality with records of selves surmounting high mountains, plumbing depths, flying to and fro. Here is evidence that we have been neither generally kind, nor compassionate, nor frugal, nor cautious. The stratum of our kind, stored as rock, in perpetuity, our moment, will be discoloured, in a way that no stratum has ever been. It will be stained with the indelible trace of evil.

Or not. For there is kindness, and valour, and dignified silence. There have been children saved from the flames and populaces delivered from starvation. There has been the tenderness of lovers and of last moments, there has been long and patient study, and the nursing of the sick. So too have artists make marks, and those marks have been reverenced, sometimes in archives.

But for me, most affectingly, there has been Natalia Akerman's face as recorded by her daughter Chantal. That may be a talisman of infinite potential.

The Kingdom of Angels

Visits to the BFI National Archive were made always in the shadow of Chantal Akerman's sudden death. Her disappearance had preoccupied me for some time. By contrast, I knew little of Stuart Croft's work, and so the fact of his death emerged only as I worked through his archived documents. One death had followed another, the experience of one interacting with discovery of another, as if strands of genetic material unwound and coalesced to form a new sequence, unpredictable and novel. I had hoped to experience a change of heart, and find peaceful acceptance of loss. Yet the work seems to have had the reverse effect. A tight knot was made tighter. Thoughts of separation, loss and mass extinction imposed themselves by turns. Chantal Akerman had in life presented to me the possibility of a limitless encounter with the *other*, in whose face we might find ourselves, but who then—shockingly—took her own life. Yet her attending to her mother's face, a tiny and late scene in just a part of her body of work, has stayed with me, serving perhaps as a charm, to ward off evil.

In the year or so after her death, her departure seemed to me the beginning of a metamorphosis, of Chantal Akerman transforming into the eternal huntress, to become Artemis in the heavens perhaps. But that was idealisation, which is a denial of loss, and of death. In the cold archive room, I began to face the fact of her absence.

Stuart Croft's papers, and the marks I have studied and photographed, which have come to beguile me so, are a record of what should have been only the first half of a working life, for he died young and unexpectedly. It is tempting to imagine what the other, later half of his working life might have produced. In that case, what phantom boxes and documents might there be for me to call for? I envisage his handwriting, altered by maturity and habit, a tangible sign of the ripening of the man and the artist, whose work had evolved through long life and committed practice. The fantasy grows as I imagine that there might have emerged a late style, the work of an old man, now stripped of youthful exuberance, finding a pared-down essence, work that provides a vantage point from which to look back on early work with fresh eyes. The survey of a lifetime and a life's work invites generalisation, the mapping of a landscape, the charting of the distant contours of the land, of the chance to gaze into the blue hazy distance.

Stuart Croft wanted to make a feature film, to be called *The Kingdom of Angels*. In the last few years of his life he made many drafts of his script, and even made several trips to Los Angeles, to take meetings about financing a production. At first sight it is odd that an artist film-maker should do this, for contemporary commercial cinema seems so far removed from Stuart Croft's work and its inspirations, so varied yet so rarefied, for example Stan Douglas, Luis Buñuel, *Singin' in the Rain*, and *film noir* equally. He was a maker of artist films, looped for projection in gallery spaces. Contemporary Los Angeles, in stark contrast, is the home of the brutally commercial, of franchise fodder, CGI fantasies, and raucous comedies, work infinitely far removed even from the Hollywood of a bygone era, a cinema of relative restraint, now dwarfed by the sheer scale and sensual overload of contemporary production. What drew Stuart Croft to Los Angeles?

I imagine him taking meetings at the pool side. Against the odds he has found backing and will soon go into production. *The Kingdom of Angels* is rooted in cinema, it draws deep on the wellsprings of cinema, it plays and thinks, reconfigures and reinterprets. It is drawn from fable, dream, and the deep cross-currents of the cinema, leading the way back to a rediscovery of imagination and waking-dream. This film mines the long buried mother lode, where celluloid dreams are trapped like florid and varied life forms, preserved in the fossil realm, crystalline and lovely, which come to life by the action of light, screen and the active imagination of audiences.

I am there, a member of the audience, revelling in the deft strokes of this artist-filmmaker's brush, alive to his living, writhing cinema, a recreation and reinvention of the past, yet always in the present, as thesis and synthesis. His hand, eye, and mind make tactile contact with the mineral richness of all cinema. Here is the result. Here are patterns, circulation, and life cycles given living form, resurrecting the fossil record of all life into this ineffable moment.

I look at the convolutions of a shell revealed in a section of rock, a form that once inhabited the warm Permian seas, more than two hundred and fifty million years ago. I see a blue-print for the loops of this artist film-maker, for in a loop, past, present, and future are one.

I float among the movies I have seen or half remember. They are inchoate and lovely. I bask in the warm seas of the past, amid the myriad forms of other lives around me. I too am a fossil.

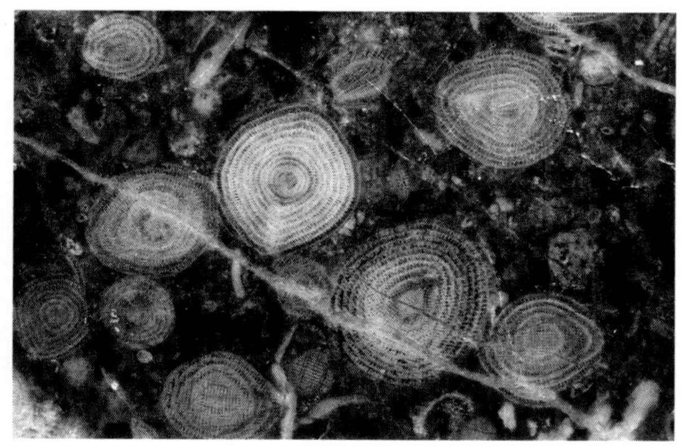

[fig. 6]

Notes

[1] *Gravity and Grace*, translated by Emma Crawford & Mario von der Ruhr, London: Routledge, 2002, p. 145 ['*Deux prisonniers, dans des cachots voisins, qui communiquent par des coups frappés contre le mur. Le mur est ce qui les sépare, mais aussi ce qui leur permet de communiquer... Toute séparation est un lien*'. Simone Weil, *La Pesanteur et la grâce*, Paris : Librairie Plon, 1947, p. 166].

[2] In Hertfordshire, England.

[3] First published 1942, then translated into English as 'Funes the Memorious', 1952. Funes complains: 'My memory, sir, is like a garbage heap,' by which he means that no detail is missing, that all experience is heaped up, unsorted. There is simply no room for generalisation or abstraction, for the normal processes of thought and memory.

[4] The film was shot in New York, in 1977. The title, in English, capitalises only the *News*, whereas *from home* is all lower case.

[5] '*Auf dem Hügel sitz ich, spähend/ In das blaue Nebelland, /Nach den fernen Triften sehend, /Wo ich dich, Geliebte, fand.*' (Lyrics by Alois Isidor Jeitteles.)

[6] '*Singen will ich, Lieder singen,/Die dir klagen meine Pein*!'

[7] Croft website: www.stuartcroft.com/comma39.shtml, accessed 10.12.19.

[8] 1952, directed by Gene Kelly and Stanley Donen.

[9] 1941, directed by Orson Welles.

[10] CRO-2-1-1 'Funding Applications'.

[11] Percy Bysshe Shelley, *Ozymandias*, 1818.

[12] A draft is in box CRO-5-6.

[13] Walter Benjamin, *The Arcades Project*, translated by Howard Eiland & Kevin McLaughlin, Cambridge, MA: Belknap Press/Harvard University Press, 1999, p. 389.

[14] That is, the illusion of an endlessly descending scale, obtained by cyclically repeating a chromatic scale made up of the superposition of sine waves separated by an octave.

[15] In Poussin's 1637–8 painting of this name, a mythological shepherd notices the shadow of his companion cast onto the stone side of a tomb, which he outlines with his finger, so discovering the art of painting. But this shadow is itself a suggestion of death, of mortality, even in Arcadia—or as Erwin Panofsky puts it, the shepherds demonstrate 'a contemplative absorption in the idea of mortality' ('*Et in Arcadia Ego*: Poussin and the Elegiac Tradition' [1936], in Erwin Panofsky, *Meaning in the Visual Arts*, Garden City, NY: Doubleday Anchor Books, 1955.

[16] Also known as *American Stories, Food, Family and Philosophy*.

[17] Translating a song for Akerman's documentary *Dis-moi* of 1980 in such a dialect required finding the right person, which only happened by luck. It was otherwise unintelligible to other Yiddish speakers.

[18] George Steiner, *Language and Silence. Essays on Language, Literature and the Inhuman*, Newhaven, CT: Yale University Press, 1967, p. 123.

[19] UK national grid reference NR8387910.

Image sources and credits

Fig. 1
Photo: Adam Roberts, with permission of Stuart Croft Foundation & BFI National Archive

Fig. 2
Photo: Adam Roberts, with permission of Stuart Croft Foundation & BFI National Archive

Fig. 3
Main négative rouge, Grotte de Chauvet-Pont-d'Arc © J. Monney / MC. Courtesy of Centre National de Préhistoire, Périgueux

Fig. 4
Frame from *News from home*, courtesy of Sylviane Franco

Fig. 5
Photo: Adam Roberts, with permission of Stuart Croft Foundation & BFI National Archive

Fig. 6
Neoschwagerina craticulifera fossil, foraminifera, in Upper Permian rock section © Universal Images Group North America LLC / DeAgostini / Alamy Stock Photo

Cover image
Rock strata, Karijini National Park, Western Australia © George Clerk

Acknowledgements

I would like to thank Henty Bulley for her invaluable, generous help and advice with this text. I would like to thank the Stuart Croft Foundation for the bursary that made this research and writing possible, in particular Steven Eastwood, friend of Stuart Croft's and Trustee of the Foundation. Thanks are also due to Emma Bennet and Harriet Fleuriot. The BFI National Archive was wonderfully hospitable, and I am grateful to archivists Wendy Russell and Fabian Macpherson. Gareth Evans and Louise Lyon have helped this text find its way with marvellous generosity. I am grateful for the kind permission given to me for inclusion of images by Chantal Akerman's sister Sylviane Franco, by the Stuart Croft Foundation, and by the Centre National de Préhistoire. I also thank Gerard Bell and Keira Greene for their inspiration and support. I would also like to express my sincere gratitude to MA BIBLIOTHÈQUE and its founder Sharon Kivland.